A PLAY

9 Never Saw Another Butterfly

by

CELESTE RASPANTI

THE DRAMATIC PUBLISHING COMPANY
CHICAGO

TO RAJA

SOME INTRODUCTORY NOTES

From 1942 to 1945 over 15,000 Jewish children passed through Terezin, a former military garrison set up as a ghetto. It soon became a station, a stopping-off place, for hundreds of thousands on their way to the gas chambers of Auschwitz. When Terezin was liberated in May, 1945, only about one hundred children were alive to return to what was left of their lives, their homes and families. The story of those years at Terezin remains in drawings and poems collected and published in the book, I Never Saw Another Butterfly.

The appendix to I Never Saw Another Butterfly briefly notes the names of the children, the dates of their birth and transportation to Terezin. For most of the children whose work appears in the book, the brief biography ends, "perished at Auschwitz. . . ." But one child, Raja Englanderova, "after the liberation, returned to Prague." This play is an imaginative creation of her story from documentary materials: poems, diaries, letters, journals, drawings and pictures.

The play and its production have come into existence only with the interest and assistance of: Karel Lagus, Curator of the Jewish Museum in Prague; Robert G. Pitman, creator and director of the first production; and Walter J. Johannsen, a personal friend. Each will recognize his part in this work and, hopefully, accept the author's sincerest gratitude.

I NEVER SAW ANOTHER BUTTERFLY

A Play

For Four Men, Seven Women, and Four Children*

CHARACTERS

RAJA ENGLANDEROVA............ *from Terezin*

FATHER
MOTHER ⎤ ....*her parents*

VERA.................................. *her aunt*

PAVEL............................. *her brother*

ERIKA.............................. *a neighbor*

IRENA SYNKOVA..................... *a teacher*

RENKA............................. *her assistant*

IRCA............................. *Pavel's fiancée*

HONZA.......................... *a friend of Raja*

RABBI.............................. *at Terezin*

CHILD I
CHILD II
CHILD III ⎤ ....*children of Terezin*
CHILD IV

LOUDSPEAKER .... *a voice*

THE YOUTH OF TEREZIN

---

*A variable number of children and young people may participate, although only four have speaking parts.

5

9 Never Saw Another Butterfly

(An open stage. Projection screen. The stage is
set with various levels and steps. As the house
dims and the music comes up, butterflies are
projected over the entire stage area. [See production notes.] The music grows in intensity until a train whistle in the distance drowns it out.
As the train sound increases, the butterflies
disappear. As the train sound fades, lights
come up on RAJA, who stands downstage facing
the audience. She is carrying a school bag and
a bundle whose outer covering is a black shawl.)

RAJA. My name is Raja. I was born in Prague. I
am a Jew--and I survived Terezin. (She sets
down her belongings, sits down and removes her
scarf, looking out over the audience.)
LOUDSPEAKER. Zuzana Winterova, 11 years old--
perished at Auschwitz, October 4, 1944.
Gabriela Freiova, 10 years old--perished at
Auschwitz, May 18, 1944. Frantisek Brozan,
14 years old--perished at Auschwitz, December
15, 1943. Eva Bulova, 15 years old--perished
at Auschwitz, October 4, 1944. Liana Frank-
lova, 13 years old--perished at Auschwitz,
October 19, 1944. Alfred Weisskopf, 16 years
old--perished at Auschwitz, December 18, 1944.
Honza--Honza Kosek, 16 1/2 years old--per-
ished at Auschwitz, January 21, 1945 . . .
RAJA (stands to face in the direction of the voice;

she walks slowly downstage and speaks). My
name--is Raja. I was born in Prague. Father,
Mother, Pavel, Irca--Irena, Honza--they are
all gone, and I am alone. But that is not im-
portant. Only one thing is important--that I
am a Jew, and that I survived. Terezin was a
fortress built by Emperor Joseph II of Austria
for his mother Maria Teresa. About sixty kilo-
meters from Prague it slept quietly in its green
valley under blue skies until . . .
LOUDSPEAKER (an arrogant, military voice, interrupting). March 5, 1939. German Wehr-
macht enters Prague. (Martial music under
the following announcements.) December 1,
1939. Jewish children excluded from state
elementary schools. June 14, 1940. Auschwitz
concentration camp set up. September 27, 1941.
Reinhard Heydrich orders mass deportation of
Jews and establishes Terezin as a Jewish ghetto.
October 16, 1941. (Train sounds start and accel-
erate.) First transports leave Prague for
Terezin. (Train sounds.) Among them were
children . . .

(Train noises die down as light flashes on in upstage area. IRENA SYNKOVA, one of the first
inhabitants of Terezin, stands in the light with
her back to the audience. She is holding a sheaf
of odd-sized papers. She is a strong woman; one
knows this by her voice and by the way she evokes
strength in others. She has taken responsibility
for the children in the camp, organized them into groups, planned lessons in a makeshift school
for them. She is obsessed with their survival,
and the survival in them of what is best. RENKA,
a young woman who assists IRENA with the
school and the care of the children, speaks from

the darkness.)

RENKA. Irena, Irena Synkova--it's Renka. . . .
IRENA. Here--in the back. (She approaches the
     outer rim of the dark circle that circumscribes
     the classroom. She extends her hand to
     RENKA.) Have the children arrived?
RENKA (coming into the light, followed by a small
     group of children). Yes, nearly four hundred--
     more than the earlier transport. (She turns to
     the children who are now surrounding her, speak-
     ing warmly and kindly.) Come, come along--
     we'll go with the others.
IRENA. Later, when the workers return--and the
     older children, we'll find places for them in the
     barracks--each one must have a place.
RENKA. And tomorrow, when another trainload
     arrives?
IRENA. We'll find a place for them--in the bar-
     racks and--(With determination.)--here in the
     school. They must start living again. (To the
     children huddled around RENKA.) School--
     yes, you will go to school again. . . . But go
     along now with Renka . . . to the bathhouse and
     then supper. . . . I promise . . .
RENKA. Come. (She leads the group off. They
     seem to walk more quickly now.)

(RAJA, who has been watching from the distance,
     steps out of the area and takes her place in line
     with the children. IRENA has returned to fold-
     ing and arranging papers when she notices the
     child.)

IRENA. You must go along now to the bathhouse,
     dear. (RAJA remains tense, staring. There
     is a shrill, siren-like sound. She sits on the

ground clutching her bag to her, following the
children with her eyes.)

RAJA. They told Papa, "Come along now to the
bathhouse . . . you must take a shower so that
we don't get any sickness in the camp." They
told him to leave his clothes in the yard on the
ground in front of him. They told him to put his
shoes next to his clothes so he could find them
again . . . but they took him to the gas . . . he
never got his shoes . . .

IRENA (walking to her). Don't be afraid. (She sees
that RAJA is staring after the children.) This
is a real bathhouse.   You can have soap and take
a shower.

RAJA (pulling away, frightened). They took him to
the bathhouse--he never got his shoes . . .

IRENA (finally understanding). That was Auschwitz.
Here you are with friends. What is your name?
(RAJA shakes her head and pulls away.) I am
Irena Synkova. I'm a teacher here in Terezin.
You'll come to school with us, won't you? (RAJA
turns and drops to the floor, covering her face
with her hands. IRENA kneels at a distance from
her, talking very quietly.) You are from Prague?
I once taught in Prague. It's a beautiful city.
When I first came to Prague, I was about your
age. I remember how frightened I was. But
after I made some friends, I was happy to live
there. Now you are not alone, and you must not
be afraid either. (She reaches for her gently.
At the first touch, the child recoils, but does
not move away. She allows IRENA to remove her
scarf and to take the sack from her clenched fist.
She watches IRENA'S face.) Now that you know
my name, you must tell me yours. How can we
be friends? I won't know what to call you.

RAJA. My number is tattooed here. (Still watching

her, RAJA stretches out her arm and shows a
number tattooed on her arm. IRENA, touched
by this, caresses her arm gently and smooths
her hair. She begins to look through the pack
and finds an identification tag.)

IRENA (reading the tag).   Raja Englanderova.
(RAJA watches silently as IRENA carefully re-
places the tattered clothes, the box, etc. in her
pack. IRENA rises.)   Come, Raja, Raja
Englanderova.   Let me tell you about our school.
(When the child does not respond, IRENA walks
to the side and kneels to sort the papers she had
with her.   She is very much aware that RAJA is
watching her.)   There's so much to do here in
school.   You will be coming here, tomorrow,
perhaps.   There are many children here. We
have few books--but we have many songs: every
day if you wish, you may paint and draw; here,
see, each of the children has drawn a spring
picture.   Would you like to paint? I'll find some
paper for you, then tomorrow--you may begin.
(RAJA has been watching IRENA from a kneel-
ing position.   She rises slowly and walks up behind IRENA, who is busily sorting and folding
papers.)   See, we save all the paper we can
find: forms, wrapping paper--and some of the
children brought their own. And when there's
enough, the children draw and paint.   Would you
like to choose a piece--of your own, Raja? (She
turns and very gently touches the child's hair,
her cheek, her arm. RAJA does not move.)

RAJA (at a level with Irena's shoulder, she timidly
imitates her action as if she were trying to con-
vince herself that this gentle person is real and
not a lie; with her hand on Irena's arm, RAJA
finally speaks).   My . . . name . . . is . . .
Raja. . . . (She leans her head wearily on

Irena's shoulder. IRENA embraces her gently.
Music.)

(Getting up slowly, RAJA turns from her past and
    returns to the lighted area downstage.)

RAJA. Slowly I began to heal, I and hundreds of
    children who passed through Irena Synkova's
    school. It was months before I could say any-
    thing but My name is Raja. I said it over and
    over to hear the sound of my voice--perhaps
    just to make sure I still knew my name--Raja.
    It was an achievement for me. Irena knew it.
    She gave me paper and paint and I wrote my
    name in stiff, crippled characters: Raja, Raja,
    Raja! It helped me to be sure I was still alive.
    One day, I suddenly wrote another name: Irena.
    Then I knew I was healed. I could paint and
    draw and speak again. I could tell Irena the
    things I was remembering. I was no longer
    afraid to remember. . . .

(RAJA turns to observe the scene upstage coming
    to life as the lights come up. She sees her
    MOTHER readying the table for the Sabbath.
    When her MOTHER calls, RAJA enters and
    takes her place in the scene.)

MOTHER (as she enters carrying the candles,
    speaking over her shoulder). Raja, cover the
    bread--and close the door to the kitchen; the
    candles will go out. . . .
RAJA (entering the scene from the darkness).
    Papa's coming up the street--Aunt Vera is
    with him. I can see them from the back window.
MOTHER (sharply). Raja, you must not open the
    back shutters. I've told you that . . . do you

hear?

(PAVEL enters.)

PAVEL. She'll get us all in trouble!
MOTHER. She'll be careful. (Calling.) Raja, come, it's time to light the Sabbath.
RAJA. Without Papa? He's coming. . . .
MOTHER. Then he will be here. Come away from the window, now.

(MOTHER turns, relieved, as FATHER and AUNT VERA enter.)

MOTHER. Papa, at last!
FATHER (with false ease). All right, Mama, all right. I'm late, but . . .
RAJA (running to him). I saw you from the window, so you weren't really late, Papa.
FATHER (kissing her and looking around at the others with a knowing look). Of course not-- as long as I am in sight, I'm not late. Besides-- I was delayed by your Aunt Vera.
AUNT VERA. I knew I would be blamed for it all. (To her sister.) It's true this time, Anna. I kept him waiting . . . you'll understand.
MOTHER (smiling, but exasperated). Of course, you would protect him. . . . (There is a kind of communication going on between the adults in the room, but an intended carelessness in their voices.)
FATHER (who has removed his coat, stepping into the center with an affectionate but tired embrace for MOTHER). Now, Anna, I'm here. (MOTHER begins to light the candles, and suddenly the room is filled with the sounds of low flying planes. They are dangerously close and

the family cringes, following the sound of each
plane as it flies over the roof. PAVEL runs to
the window to look. MOTHER quickly draws
him back.)

MOTHER.   Pavel, come away from the window.
We must keep the shutters closed . . . you
know that.

PAVEL.   Nazis. So close you can see the damned
swastikas on the wings.

MOTHER.   Pavel! The Sabbath!

PAVEL.   Sabbath Eve--and the Nazis about to join
us!

VERA.   Pavel, if you . . . if we are not careful . . .

RAJA (attentive).   They're gone now. . . .

FATHER (intently, to his son). Be careful--we
must all be careful. Tonight, the planes; tomorrow, tanks . . .

MOTHER.   Tomorrow? Josef, what do you mean?

FATHER.   Mama, Pavel--all of you. . . . (Almost in tears.) Mama, today--today, I lost
my place. . . .

MOTHER.   Josef, it can't be true. . . .

FATHER.   We all knew it had to come!

MOTHER. But you were promised!

FATHER.   Promises! What do they mean? I must
report to work at Litomerice--they are building
a station . . .

RAJA. But, Papa, you're not a carpenter. You're
a teacher.

VERA. Hush, Raja! Let your father explain. . . .

FATHER.   I must learn manual labor. Imagine--
all of us at the school--all of us.

PAVEL (contemptuously). Building a station!

FATHER.   Today they came to the school. We
were given one hour to clear away--books,
papers, everything. One hour after all those

years!

MOTHER. And the school?

VERA. Anna, wait, there is still more.

FATHER. Mama, it may be that--(PAVEL stares
at his father.)--that we will have to move--
again. . . . (Helplessly.) It may be that . . .
we must do so. The landlord is German--and
we are . . .

PAVEL (angry). Jews!

VERA. Pavel . . . try to have patience. . . .

FATHER. We . . . are . . . Jews. . . . They are
relocating the boundaries--twelve blocks on
either side--and we must all of us move into
the area of the old ghetto.

MOTHER (unbelieving). So . . . once again.

RAJA. But, Papa, they promised!

MOTHER. How soon?

FATHER. Tomorrow.

VERA. By sundown, Sabbath sundown, Anna.

PAVEL. They give us the Sabbath to get ready--
it saves a working day! What did you tell him,
Papa?

FATHER. What should I have told him? (Hopefully.) Some say it is the last order.

PAVEL. Someone always says this will be the
last order but every month the ghetto grows
smaller.

FATHER. What should I tell him? What does a
Jew tell his German landlord?

PAVEL. They can't expect us to . . .

MOTHER (trying to understand the whole impact
of the orders). And Vera?

FATHER. The women, too . . . they were re-
leased to work in the streets.

VERA. All unmarried women must report to work
in the streets . . . with the men.

PAVEL (realizing the import of this). Irca!

FATHER. Irca, too. . . . (Then gently, to
    MOTHER.) Mama, you must give up the school.
    Jews are no longer allowed to teach. . . .
PAVEL. Irca? Where is she?
FATHER. They were turned out in the streets--
    with the rest.
PAVEL. But we thought the Council was going to
    appeal? Why does the Council sit waiting while
    the whole Nazi army walks in?
FATHER. There have been . . . meetings.
PAVEL. Talk!
FATHER. There are--considerations. . . . (He
    is beginning to show his anger.) So, you will
    attack, shout slogans, you--and your friends--
    (Derisively.)--be brave!
PAVEL. Better than hiding behind our prayer
    shawls! (FATHER rises, affronted, and stands
    staring at PAVEL.)
MOTHER. Pavel, you go too far.
PAVEL. At least shouting lets the Nazis know
    we're alive.
FATHER. You go too far . . . too far. . . . (He
    is limp with controlling his anger. He sits
    wearily and then turns to speak directly to
    PAVEL.) You think we don't know--last night,
    your joke, at the Regional Theatre . . .
MOTHER (looking at her son). The Regional
    Theatre? Pavel, you know Jews are not allowed
    to . . .
PAVEL. A little joke on the guards. (Cautiously,
    to his father.) What do you know? (With uneasy
    bravado.) So we stoned out the lights in the
    street and attacked them from ambush near the
    theatre arcade. . . . They never knew what
    happened to them. . . .
FATHER. A joke! Not so amusing this morning.
    Hanus was taken, his number called before the

rest.

PAVEL. Why Hanus?

MOTHER. Josef, you are not telling us all.

FATHER. A guard knows one of the Council. He said he recognized his son among the "pranksters."

PAVEL. But Hanus wasn't there. He didn't even know about it.

MOTHER. Pavel! It might have been you--and Papa. . . .

FATHER. The guard said he recognized him. There is no quarreling with a Nazi guard!

PAVEL. And the rest of the Council? They didn't intervene? No one protested?

FATHER (almost ashamed). Hanus is on the train now. . . .

PAVEL. Without a word! What cowards!

FATHER (near weeping with hurt anger). Pavel!

PAVEL. No wonder the star is yellow!

FATHER (striking him across the mouth). You go too far . . . too far. (He turns, ashamed.)

PAVEL (ashamed, but angry). Papa, I'm . . . sorry, but . . .

FATHER. But you do not understand . . . you cannot!

PAVEL. I understand. I have this to remind me! (Gestures to the star on his jacket.)

MOTHER (finally losing her composure). What is this talk? The star cannot destroy us--but I will tell you what can. . . . (She turns on the boy roughly.)

VERA. Anna . . . the boy doesn't know what he is saying.

MOTHER. I will tell you what can kill us. To starve! No white bread, meat, eggs, cheese, fish, poultry--fruit, jam . . .

VERA. Anna, please . . .

MOTHER. None of it--for a Jew! This will destroy us--to be denied the necessities of life . . .

PAVEL. I know, Mama . . .

MOTHER. And for your father . . . no tobacco, cigars, cigarettes, no beer--all the little pleasures taken away. . . .

PAVEL. I know that, Mama . . .

MOTHER. And the big ones, too: the school, the synagogue--this will destroy us. . . .

PAVEL. Mama, for God's sake!

MOTHER (reaching a point of exhaustion). No. I am not yet finished with being a Jew. It means for all of us separation--and the fear of separation--planes today; tanks tomorrow; and always, the guards, the Nazis! You and your foolish bravado! . . . (Breaking with her own weariness and fear.) And we may all be lost . . . all--lost.

PAVEL. I know, Mama. I see what's going on, but to just endure. It seems so . . .

FATHER. Weak? To you, it's weak. But think-- the Nazis want us to work for them! If we must work, we must eat. There's that chance for life.

PAVEL. I don't call this living!

MOTHER (recovering). But while we live, we stay together, and perhaps later . . .

FATHER. Yes . . . if they bid us work, then we will eat, and we may survive--together--this war. It cannot last much longer. . . .

PAVEL (giving in to his father's optimism). All right, Papa.

FATHER. All right, all right. So no more shouting and no more jokes on Nazi guards! In a few months we will be back in our flat. Huber has promised to keep the furniture for us--he

does not wish us harm. It will be here when we
come back.

PAVEL (wearily). Yes, Papa.

FATHER. And you and Irca will be married, as
we planned, you will see . . . I promise . . .

PAVEL (laughing wryly). Promises!

FATHER. You will see. (Cheerfully.) Come now,
Mama, the lights. (MOTHER assumes her
place at the table and begins to light the Sabbath
candles. As she does, lights dim. Searchlights
flash through the windows and light up the faces
of the group. They become tense, but MOTHER
continues the ceremony.)

MOTHER. Blessed art thou, O Lord our God, King
of the Universe, who has hallowed us by . . .

PAVEL (listening to the outside noises that have
begun to arise). The tanks . . . and guards.
They're in the street.

MOTHER. . . . His commandments and com-
manded us to . . .

PAVEL. They are starting to cordon off the street.

FATHER (resignedly). They'll be here soon.

MOTHER (continuing through the remarks). . . .
to kindle the Sabbath lights. (The room is
bright with searchlights. The outside is alive
with the sounds of tanks, marching feet. Lights
and sound reach their highest intensity as all
candles are lit. Blackout. In the darkness,
MOTHER puts out each candle slowly.)

(RAJA walks out of the group as the candles go out
one by one. She reaches the downstage area
and turns to see the last candle extinguished.
She turns again to the audience.)

RAJA. The first transports for Terezin left
Prague the next day. We waited our turn and

hoped. . . . Families moved in together. We
moved in with Irca's family, and then we moved
again. Each week another decree shrank our
ghetto--and our lives. Even then we couldn't
really believe it all. It was incredible. Our
friends lined the street and watched us leave--
five thousand Jews. . . . Erika Schlager called
to me. . . . (RAJA turns to face upstage again.)

(ERIKA appears in the dim lights upstage.)

ERIKA (calling out to RAJA across the darkness.)
Raja, Raja, where are you going? Come with
me to the cinema!

RAJA (facing her across the darkness). I can't,
Erika. We have to go to the Municipal Building.

ERIKA. But why?

RAJA. I don't know.

ERIKA. Didn't they say why?

RAJA. They say we have to go. (Lights out on
ERIKA. RAJA turns from her.) I ran ahead
to join my mother. That was the day we left
home. . . .

(A glaring light flashes on upstage to reveal Raja's
family and several children huddled together, be-
wildered.)

LOUDSPEAKER (the voice metallic and full of
authority). Jews--*Achtung!* Step quickly. Men
left! Women and children right! Keep moving.
Schnell! Schnell!

(The voice accelerates as the group of women and
children separate themselves from the men and
older boys. This group moves downstage where
IRENA is now standing.)

IRENA (gathering the children around her). Don't
be afraid. We're only going on the train. (The
following dialogue is almost simultaneous--

excited, afraid, wondering.)

CHILD I. Where's Father? What happened to
Father?

IRENA. You'll see him again at the camp. Quiet
now. We must wait.

CHILD II. It's been so long. I'm thirsty.

CHILD III. I'm hungry! Please, is there bread?

IRENA. Wait . . . wait . . . just a little while,
and we'll have plenty of food.

CHILD I. When will we be there? Will Father be
there?

IRENA (smiling encouragingly). Patience!

CHILD III. Where are we going now? What are
they doing in the room there?

IRENA. We'll see. We must wait our turn.

CHILD I. Are we going to work? They told us we
would work--together.

CHILD II. They told me to remember this number
--always.

IRENA. Yes, you must remember. At roll call,
they will ask your number. You must remember, and answer promptly.

CHILD III. They laughed and told us we were
marked, like pigs. They said--it will never go
away.

IRENA (calming them). Quiet, now. Don't be
afraid! Remember, you are not alone. Whatever you see or hear, whatever is done, remember, we are together--and then you will not
be afraid! (She walks them into a lighted area
set with steps and stools, her "classroom.")
Come, sit close together.

(The children take places on the steps and stools,
facing away from each other. They hold drawing and writing materials. They are still as
the light comes up on the group and move only

when they speak. RAJA observes them from
the distance and then, as if in a dream, she
walks through the scene, standing over each
child for a moment. Finally she returns to
the edge of the lighted area and speaks.)

RAJA. I was one of them--the children of Terezin,
one who saw everything, the barbed wire fence,
the rats, the lice, one who knew hunger, dirt
and smells, one who heard trains arrive and
leave, screaming sirens, and the tread of
heavy feet in the dark. I sat in Irena Synkova's
classroom to write and paint the story of those
days. (She takes her place in the group.)

(During the following, while the poems are being
recited, various paintings from the book I
NEVER SAW ANOTHER BUTTERFLY may be
projected on a screen.)

RAJA.
          I never saw another butterfly. . . .
          The last, the very last,
            so richly, brightly, dazzling yellow.
          Perhaps if the sun's tears sing
            against a white stone . . .
          Such, such a yellow
          Is carried lightly 'way up high.
          It went away I'm sure because it
            wished to kiss the world goodbye.
          For seven weeks I've lived in here,
          Penned up inside this ghetto,
          But I have found my people here.
          The dandelions call to me,
          And the white chestnut candles in the
            court.
          Only I never saw another butterfly.

> That butterfly was the last one.
> Butterflies don't live here in the ghetto.

CHILD II.   It is weeks since I came to this ghetto.
I did not know that such a thing could happen to
me.   When I go home, I'm going to eat only
white bread. . . .

CHILD III.   When I go home, I'm going to make
my bed every day, clean. . . .

CHILD IV.   When I go home, I'm going to drink hot
chocolate in the winter, lots of it. . . .

CHILD I.   When I go home, I'm going to have
pretty white curtains--rugs, too.

CHILD II.   I'm going to play ball in the courtyard
when I go home and shout if I want to. . . .

CHILD III.   I'm going to sit very quiet and read
story books as long as I want to when I go home--
all night maybe. . . .

CHILD IV.   I'm going to play the piano when I go
home and everyone will sing and we won't care
how noisy we are. . . .

RAJA.   When I go home . . . (She walks away from
the group and faces the audience as she speaks
her poem.)

> I've lived here in the ghetto more than a
>   year,
> In Terezin, in the black town now,
> And when I remember my old home so dear,
> I can love it more than I did, somehow.
>
> Ah, home, home,
> Why did they ever tear me away?
> Here the weak die easy as a feather.
> And when they die, they die forever.
> I'd like to go back home again,
> It makes me think of sweet spring flowers.
> Before, when I used to live at home,

It never seemed so dear and fair.

CHILD I (interrupting RAJA as she speaks her
    last line). Everything here is so strange--
    different from anywhere else in the world.

CHILD II. People walk on the street, not just on
    the sidewalk. But there are so many of us here
    that we wouldn't fit on the sidewalk. Cars do not
    drive here, though, so nothing can run over us.

CHILD III. We sleep in bunks, and everywhere
    lots of people are packed in.

CHILD IV. Mothers and fathers don't live together
    and children live away from them in homes, or
    whatever you call it.

CHILD I (wistfully). When you hear the word home,
    you imagine something quite nice. Well, here
    it's all quite different. . . .

CHILD III.
        The buildings now are fuller,
        Body smelling close to body,
        The garrets scream with light for long,
            long hours.

CHILD IV.
        This evening I walked along the street of
            death.
        On one wagon, they were taking the dead
            away.

CHILD III. I haven't seen my mother for so long--I
    don't even know if she has arrived. Irena says
    that somewhere, she is looking for me; if I stay
    here, and keep well, she will find me. I wonder
    where she is . . . and Father . . . and Grandpa.
    He told me to wait for him at the station, but
    they wouldn't let me. I think, maybe, he never
    came at all.

CHILD II. I have never been away from home before, not even over the holidays because I have
no aunt or uncle to visit in the country. So this
is my first trip away from my parents. It's so
strange. . . . I've learned here to appreciate
ordinary things that, if we had them when we
were still free, we didn't notice them at all.
Like riding a bus or a train, or walking freely
along a road, to the water, say. Or to go to
buy ice cream. Such an ordinary thing is out of
our reach. . . .

CHILD III.

In Terezin in the so-called park
A queer old granddad sits
Somewhere in the so-called park.
He wears a beard down to his lap
And on his head a little cap.
Hard crusts he crumbles in his gums,
He's only got one single tooth.
Instead of soft rolls, lentil soup.
Poor old greybeard.

CHILD I. May I call you "grandfather"? You have
no little girl and I have no grandpa.

RAJA. Tuesday, March 16, 1943. Today I went to
see my uncle in the Sudeten barracks, and there
I saw them throw potato peelings and people
threw themselves on the little piles and fought
for them.

CHILD II. Tuesday, April 6, 1943. Tomorrow the
SS men are coming and no children can go out on
the street. Daddy won't know this and I'll die of
hunger by evening. . . . Wednesday, April 7,
1943. I missed Daddy yesterday, but I didn't
cry. The other children couldn't see their
parents either. . . .

CHILD III. We aren't allowed to go out of the

barracks. We can't go out in the streets without a pass and children don't get a pass. They say this can last a week or even months . . . like a bird in a cage . . .

RAJA. Last night I had a beautiful dream. I was home; I saw our flat and our street. Now I am disappointed and out of sorts, because I awoke in the bunk instead of my own bed. This isn't a home any more, it's a hospital. Everyone avoids us; half the children are sick in bed . . . the number of the sick goes up every day. Rooms full of patients, and the doctor does not know what to do.

CHILD III. Typhoid raged through Terezin. The hospitals and infirmaries are crowded. They cleared out a whole house and made a typhoid ward of it. Everywhere you see the sign: *Achtung, Tyfus!* At every water faucet and pump, Don't forget to wash your hands. But anyway, the water hardly ever runs.

CHILD I. I caught six fleas and three bedbugs today. Isn't that a fine hunt? I don't need a gun and right away I have supper. A rat slept in my shoe. Walter, our Hausaltester, killed it. Now I'm going to pitch a tent for the night with Eva.

RAJA. It's terrible here now. There is a great deal of tension among the older children. They are going to send transports to the new ghetto-- into the unknown. And fifteen hundred children will arrive tonight. They are from Poland. We are making toys, little bags and nets for them.

CHILD III. They came yesterday. No one was allowed near them. But we managed to get some news from the barracks. None of the children can speak Czech, we don't even know if they are Jewish children or Polish or what. You can see them a little from the fortress wall, and they went in the morning to the reception center.

CHILD I. They look awful. You can't guess how
old they are, they all have old faces and tiny
bodies. They are all barelegged and only a very
few have shoes. They returned from the reception center with their heads shaved. They have
lice. They all have such frightened eyes.

RAJA.
> The poor thing stands there vainly.
> Vainly he strains his voice.
> Perhaps he'll die. Then can you say
> How beautiful is the world today?

CHILD II. We got used to standing in line at 7
o'clock in the morning, at 12 noon and again
at 7 o'clock in the evening. We stood in a long
line with a plate in our hand, and they gave us
a little warmed-up water with a salty or coffee
flavor. Or else they gave us a few potatoes.
We got used to sleeping without a bed, to salut-
ing every uniform, not walk on the sidewalks
and then again to walk on the sidewalks. We got
used to undeserved slaps, blows and executions.
We got used to seeing people die in their own
excrement, to seeing piled-up coffins full of
corpses, to seeing the sick amidst dirt and filth
and to seeing the helpless doctors. We got used
to it that from time to time, one thousand unhappy souls would come here and that, from
time to time, another thousand unhappy souls
would go away. . . . (Distant train noises.)

CHILD I. Sunday, September 5, 1943. This was
the day, but it's all over now. They are already
in the train. From our room Pavla, Helena,
Olila and Popinka are going.

CHILD III. Everyone gave Olila something, she
is such a poor thing. At six this evening they

reported for the transport. Each one somewhere
else. The parting was hard.

RAJA. Monday, September 6, 1943. I got up at
six to see Zdenka. When I came up to the barracks the last people were just going through
the back gates and getting on the train. Everything was boarded up all around so no one could
get to them and so they could not run away. I
jumped over, ran up to the last people going
through the gates. I saw the train pulling away
and in one of the cars Zdenka was riding. (Train
noises up and out.)

(RAJA looks up from her reading when she hears
the train. She sees lights come up on another
acting area and she recognizes the scene. She
rises and takes her role in that memory. When
she speaks there is an adult bitterness in her
voice.)

RAJA. Where did Zdenka go?
IRENA. The transport--to the East . . .
RAJA. Why?
IRENA. To work . . . resettlement . . . to . . .
RAJA (interrupting). Auschwitz.
IRENA. Auschwitz?
RAJA (turning away and sitting wearily, with an old
sigh). She will not come back. Jiri told us. And
he knows. You die if you go to Auschwitz.
IRENA. Raja . . .
RAJA. It is true. I know. You die, and the ovens
and the chimneys--when you die, you burn to
ashes . . .
IRENA. We do not know this is true.
RAJA. I know. And you know, too. And you think
because we are children that we do not know. . . .
IRENA (slowly realizing Raja's awareness). What

have you heard. Where?

RAJA. Jiri told us; he came from Warsaw. You
die if you go to Auschwitz. And no one returns.
Every day--the trains go--and no one returns.
Jiri was there. He escaped. He told us. How
is it that you do not know?

IRENA (quietly). I've heard the same talk--we all
have. It can't be true. Think, Raja, such things
can't be true.

RAJA. But it is--he told us--we are going to die.

IRENA. Raja--wait--you are only afraid . . .
wait . . .

RAJA (pleading with her, really frightened). Irena--
I want to go home--I hate this place--and everything. . . .

IRENA. Everything? . . .

RAJA. Yes, what's the use of anything if we are
going to die? Zdenka--last night we shared our
bread and sang together--and now she is gone.

IRENA. I know. . . . (These lines are almost
simultaneous.)

RAJA. And Eva and Miriam and Marianna . . .

IRENA. I miss them, too. . . .

RAJA. Gabriela and Zuzana . . .

IRENA. I know . . . I know. . . .

RAJA. We'd promised--we'd keep together--that
next year in Prague--we'd go to school--to-
gether. Now there is nothing left.

IRENA. They were your friends. You loved them.
Do not forget how you worked together--in this
very room--and the poems, and the songs. Eva,
Zuzana and Gabriela--their pictures, see . . .

RAJA (snatching them away). No. They will burn
them, too! (She tries to rip them.)

IRENA (retrieving the pictures and holding Raja's
arms). Raja, listen to me. You are no longer
a child--this minute, you are no longer a child--

and so I tell you. . . . (She gently forces RAJA
to sit down and, holding her hands, continues.)
I have a child--she is nine years old--she was
torn away from my arms and thrown from the
train by an angered guard. I tried to throw my-
self after her--but I was dragged back into the
car. I wanted to die until I came to Terezin
and found thousands of children waiting for me--
and then I knew I must not die. . . . Do you
understand? (RAJA has listened, stunned but
calmed. She turns away.) You are no longer a
child--and so I tell you. I have a child and she
lives whenever I comfort another child or dry
her tears. (RAJA turns away in despair. IRENA
stands waiting helplessly but tenderly. IRENA
opens her arms and RAJA, in a gesture that re-
calls their first meeting, puts her head on Irena's
shoulder and weeps. She rises with a new-found
strength and walks downstage as the lights go
down on the scene.)

(Lights come up on RAJA, who is sitting DL. She
is an older child, the RAJA of the liberation.
She addresses the audience.)

RAJA.   Fear--this is half the story of Terezin--
its beginning, but not its end. I was a child
there, I knew that word. I became a woman
there because I learned another word from Irca
and Pavel, from Father and Mother, from Irena
Synkova. I learned the word "courage" and
found the determination to live--to believe in
life. . . .

        (Lights come up on IRCA and PAVEL.)

IRCA.   I believe in life . . . I and Pavel. (She

goes to PAVEL and takes his hand.) Pavel, I
am coming with you. I settled everything my-
self, and I have a number in your transport.
PAVEL. Your mother and father need you. Go
back to the barracks.
IRCA. Pavel, you are closer to me than parents.
I must come with you! (PAVEL, taking her
hand, walks toward the edge of the circle of
light and calls quietly.)
PAVEL. Rabbi, we want . . . Could you marry us,
Rabbi?

(The RABBI appears at the edge of the lighted area.)

RABBI. I can. Have you . . . a wedding ring?
PAVEL. Yes.
RABBI. How much time?
PAVEL. An hour at most.
RABBI. That will be enough. Tell me your Hebrew
names . . . and we must call your parents and
some friends.

(Slowly a few PEOPLE [this group includes
the members of Pavel's family] enter as if to
a great ceremony. A ritual canopy is brought
in and held over the young couple. With as
much of the ritual as possible, simple and
touching in a makeshift way, a traditional Jewish
wedding is performed. The group surrounds
the couple as the RABBI addresses them.)

RABBI. Dearly Beloved, in the Bible we read
three words, the meaning of which we have
never understood as well as today. They are:
Lekh, red, vealita--go, lower yourself, and
you will rise. We too have sunk very low but
risen very high, because we did not let our sad

fate overwhelm us; we have not lost hope that
right will finally be victorious over injustice,
friendship over hostility, love over hatred,
peace over war. If these terrible times had not
come, you two young people might not have met
and loved and decided to share your lives. And
so you may say--good may arise out of evil.
(The RABBI blesses them and intones the Psalm.
As the Psalm continues, members of the group
come to the young couple with their greetings.)

> Happy those who live in your house
>   and praise you all day long;
> Happy the pilgrims inspired by you
>   with courage to make the journey.
> As they walk through the Valley of Sorrow,
>   they make it a place of springs. . . .
> Yahweh Sabaoth, hear my prayer,
>   Listen, God of Jacob;
> God our shield, now look on us
>   and be kind to your anointed.
> For God is battlement and shield
>   conferring grace and glory;
> Adonoi withholds nothing good
>   from those who walk without blame.
> As they walk through the Valley of Sorrow,
>   they make it a place of springs. . . .

(He blesses the cup of wine.) Blessed art Thou,
O Lord our God, King of the universe, who hast
created the fruit of the vine. (He gives the cup
to PAVEL, who drinks. PAVEL then gives it
to IRCA. After she drinks she returns the cup
to AUNT VERA, who is standing by. MOTHER
takes off her wedding ring and gives it to PAVEL
with a quiet gesture of affection. He places the
ring on IRCA'S forefinger. He repeats after the
RABBI:)
PAVEL.   Thou art consecrated to me with this ring

as my wife, according to the faith of Moses and
Israel. (The wedding couple and the RABBI ex-
change positions.   The RABBI then pronounces
the priestly benediction.)

RABBI. May the Lord bless you and protect you;
may the Lord show you favor and be gracious to
you.   May the Lord turn in loving kindness to
you and grant you peace. Amen. (The tallis is
removed. AUNT VERA steps forward and pre-
sents PAVEL with a glass and a kerchief. He
wraps the kerchief around the glass, places it
on the floor and steps on it. "The breaking of
the glass" is intended to temper the joy of the
occasion by reminding those present of the de-
struction of the Temple in Jerusalem and of
other calamities that befell the Jewish people.
At the moment PAVEL breaks the glass, the
sound of an approaching train is heard. One by
one the crowd exit.)

RAJA (who has been watching from a distance, now
turning to the audience). One by one the transports came. Mother, Father, Aunt Vera--they
went. Pavel and Irca--they went. Everyone I
knew and loved in Prague. There was no one who
could remember me before I had come here as a
child of twelve . . . but there were many left
standing at the train as the transports started
up, the cars crowded, boarded, sealed. . . .

(Sound of train departing is heard. RAJA follows
the sound as it leaves. As her eyes move across
the stage she sees HONZA. He turns to her.)

RAJA. And we turned and found each other. . . .
HONZA (staring after the train). Jiri--they said
they wouldn't take him. He was a plumber, an
electrician--so clever--they said they wouldn't

take him. . . .

RAJA. Everyone goes. . . . Jiri? Was he your
friend?

HONZA (turning). He was my brother. . . .

RAJA. You're Honza Kosek. I heard about you.
My name is Raja--Raja Englanderova. My
brother . . . Pavel . . . and Irca . . .

HONZA. I know . . . they just got married, and
now . . . what's the good of that?

RAJA (turning away, a little angry). They're still
together.

HONZA. What's the good of that!

RAJA. Together they'll not be afraid. That's the
good!

HONZA (embarrassed). You are afraid.

RAJA. What if I am? You're laughing at me . . .
you think I'm a coward. . . .

HONZA. I'm laughing at you because you're a girl,
and don't know the first thing about--about anything.

RAJA. Well . . . it's all easy for you. I've heard
how you get by the guards--it's easy for a boy.

HONZA. Maybe. (He touches her shoulder almost
tenderly and turns her around to face him.) My
father was beaten and left for dead before my
eyes. I saw it. I couldn't move, I was so afraid.
But I didn't run. I never understood it--until my
father dying told me, "You're a good boy, Honza:
you are afraid, but you are not a coward."

RAJA (ashamed). I'm sorry. . . . (Reluctantly.)
Well, it's late. . . . I have to go. . . .

HONZA. Where're you going?

RAJA. Number twenty-five. . . . Where do you
live?

HONZA. House Number two--on the other side,
near the wall.

RAJA (eager to talk). There're thirty girls--in our

group--most of us from Prague. . . . Irena . . .
she's in charge of the whole compound--she lives
with us.

HONZA. We live alone; we elect our own leader--
and we have meetings--secret ones.

RAJA. Don't you have one of the older men there?

HONZA. What for? We're all old enough--we work
in the fields. . . .

RAJA. So do we--some of us. I do. I'm old
enough.

HONZA. We take care of everything ourselves.
I'm the leader now--I was elected. So I'm in
charge.

RAJA. Don't you go to school--at night, after
work?

HONZA. We do--sometimes. Sometimes we have
meetings--the leaders from the boys' homes--
and we talk and plan. . . .

RAJA. What?

HONZA. Oh, like someone gets an idea about
something and we talk about it--or someone does
something we don't like and we tell him to quit
it or else. A lot of things. We're working on
something right now.

RAJA. For the boys' home?

HONZA. Well, not just for the boys--we're going
to have a newspaper and report the news in camp.

RAJA. Have you got a printing press?

HONZA. No--we don't need that. It's not that kind
of a paper. We make copies of the news and hang
them around in the barracks. It's my idea. . . .

RAJA. Will you put one in the girls' home?

HONZA. I suppose we could--I never thought about
it.

RAJA. I'd copy it over--I could do that.

HONZA. I'd have to talk about it with the rest. I
suppose it's a good idea. . . . Well, I guess I've

got to go now--we're going to have a meeting
about the paper. (He walks away, and then
turns, shrugging a shoulder at her.) You can
come if you want to. (She hesitates, and then
runs to him.)

(Lights go down as RAJA walks downstage, speaking to the audience.)

RAJA. And so VEDEM was born--and lived for
three years, and helped us live. We waited to
read the copy posted in our barracks, and later
when, for safety, it was read aloud, no one was
missing. It was an invisible line of communication between the houses so that even across
the dark yards and crowded barracks, the youth
of Terezin grew up together.
HONZA (calling from the darkness to RAJA, who
has just finished speaking). Raja? (Lights up
on his area when she enters.)
RAJA. Yes? I can only stay a few minutes. Is
this week's VEDEM ready?
HONZA. Here it is. . . .
RAJA. I'll take it and get started. (She turns.)
HONZA. Wait. . . . I was thinking. . . . We've
talked about it at the meeting . . . we could run
some of the poems from the girls' house--when
there's room.
RAJA. Good. Irena will be glad of that. She said
it might happen. The smaller girls got all ex-
cited!
HONZA. There won't be room for too many. . . .
RAJA. I'll tell her. (She turns to leave, almost
reluctantly.) I'll see you. . . .
HONZA. Wait. . . . I saw you in the field today.
Of course I couldn't say anything.
RAJA. I know. I saw you--across the road.

HONZA. Maybe we could plan a way to meet there
    --in case . . . there are messages . . . or any-
    thing.
RAJA. It wouldn't be safe! The guards are every-
    where.
HONZA. We meet here . . . at night.
RAJA. The guards think we're inside the barracks.
HONZA. I'm not afraid . . . are you?
RAJA. No . . . yes, I guess I am. They'd beat
    you.
HONZA. It wouldn't be the first time. I always get
    up again. . . .
RAJA. Some day . . .
HONZA. Some day, maybe, I won't, I suppose.
    What difference does it make?
RAJA. Don't talk like that. I'll go if you do.
    (Starts to leave.)
HONZA. Wait . . . wait. I'm only teasing.
RAJA. It would be lonesome without you. I mean,
    the boys need you, and the paper. Irena says
    you're the only one she can trust to bury the
    drawings and the poems.
HONZA. Others would do that. . . .
RAJA. It would be hard . . . I mean . . . these
    months we've been good friends. . . . I'd miss
    you too. (She walks over to his side.)
HONZA (after a silence; taking her hand). I meant
    to say that first.
RAJA. I know. (They walk together in silence,
    hand in hand, to the edge of the lighted area.)
    Good night. . . .
HONZA. Good night. (They separate and run to
    other lighted areas. Turning away, they speak
    to each other across the darkness.) Raja, Raja!
RAJA. Yes. . . .
HONZA. I have some flowers for you.
RAJA. Honza, if you get caught . . .

HONZA. You know the square in front of the
  tower . . .
RAJA. The prisoners aren't allowed there. . . .
HONZA. I know, but they can't stop us from looking at it. Look, from here . . . see the flowers
  near the corner--and the butterflies? . . .
RAJA. I see them. . . .
HONZA. Well, I'm giving them to you, and every
  time you pass . . .
RAJA. I'll say--they're mine. Honza gave them
  to me--all the flowers--and all the butterflies.
  Thank you, oh, thank you. . . . (They turn into
  another lighted area.) Honza, Irena gave me a
  book of poetry--I left it for you at the end of the
  field near the shed. I want you to read one special poem. . . .
HONZA. I found it--and read it--and left one for
  you . . . look for it. (They hold hands and run
  together into another area.) Raja, look. . . .
RAJA (holding a small package). What is it?
HONZA. Open it--careful--it's very expensive.
RÁJA. It must be--since you crawled through the
  barracks to bring it. Why didn't you leave it in
  the shed?
HONZA. It can't be left--not around here.
RAJA (opening package slowly, pulling out a sau-
  sage). Honza, a sausage--you're wonderful--
  and sausage, I haven't--but where did you get it?
HONZA. I liberated it. . . .
RAJA. Liberated it? Honza . . .
HONZA. Actually, I took it.
RAJA (biting one end, then handing him the other).
  Stole it. No wonder it tastes so good--you're
  so brave! (They hold hands and run together to
  another area.)
HONZA (haltingly). I won't be here--for a few
  days . . .

RAJA. Why? Where are you going?

HONZA. Don't take any chances--coming to meet me, I mean.

RAJA (frightened). Honza, what is it?

HONZA. Nothing. A special detail to build something outside the fortifications. They're picking the strongest--I'll be chosen.

RAJA. But--what if something happens?

HONZA. There'll be a chance for extra food. (Smiles.) Maybe another sausage.

RAJA. I don't care about the sausage. . . . Honza, I'm afraid!

HONZA. Don't worry . . . they want the job done-- it's some kind of walled courtyard . . . nothing much can happen. . . . Well, I have to go.

RAJA (reluctantly, almost angrily). Good-bye then. . . . (They walk together to the edge of the lighted area. HONZA walks into the darkness.) Good-bye. I'll be waiting . . . waiting. . . . Please come back. (She sits with her head in her hands.)

(IRENA calls from a lighted area a distance away.)

IRENA. Raja, Raja, it's all right. A message came through.

RAJA (growing tense). What is it? Tell me. Tell me.

IRENA. The boys are back . . . all of them!

RAJA (coming to her). I've been holding my breath for two days . . . waiting . . . waiting . . . I couldn't think of anything else but Honza!

IRENA. What would you have done if he had not come back? If weeks and months had passed?

RAJA. Waited . . . and held my breath . . . for tomorrow . . . then waited again.

IRENA. Waiting days are long days, Raja. You

would learn to stop thinking of tomorrow and to
keep alive today. That's the secret of waiting--
remember that--to keep alive today.

RAJA. Part of me would always be waiting.

IRENA. Then you would do what we all learn to do
to make waiting bearable.

RAJA. I don't know how . . . I'm afraid. . . .

IRENA. Afraid of tomorrow? Then think of today--
now. Can you live until tonight?

RAJA (puzzled). Yes. . . .

IRENA (intensely). And tomorrow morning . . . do
you think you can live till noon?

RAJA. Yes. . . .

IRENA. And at noon, in the heat and the hunger,
the stench and the weariness . . . can you live
until night?

RAJA. Yes, yes. . . .

IRENA. Then you will survive. Each day you find
some reason . . .

RAJA (aware of Irena's meaning). As you have
done.

IRENA. Yes. Somehow--one of us is sure to survive. One of us must teach the children how to
sing again, to write on paper with a pencil, to do
sums and draw pictures. So we survive each today. . . . (Lights down on scene.)

RAJA (walking to the edge of the stage). The singing, the reading, the learning--the poetry and
the drawings--this was part of our survival. In
spite of the SS Guards and the orders against
teaching, Irena kept school in the children's
barracks. An older boy was always on guard
and at sight of the SS men he whistled, and
teaching turned into children's games. Games
were permitted, but learning was a crime--for
Jews. (She sits down. Lights come up on another area where the CHILDREN are dancing

and singing in mime.) We had books. Each of us
had brought at least one book with him. Profes-
sional musicians, actors and singers brought
their repertoire with them. Irena brought
Ludvik, the children's opera, with her and she
did it with the children. (The music of Ludvik
comes up. Over the music, Raja's voice.) In
Terezin Ludvik was one of the things one had to
see. Thousands heard its melodies, hundreds
of children experienced in the rehearsals and
performances the strongest impressions of
their short lives. . . . (She turns to watch the
children as they pantomime the opera with suit-
able makeshift costumes and gestures.) The
story was an old one--the legend of the birds of
Cheb and the villain, Ludvik the Carpenter, who
hated them because of their song. (In the pantomime HONZA enters as a villain and begins to
build cages.) He built boxes and cages for the
birds and trapped them one by one until Cheb
lay sad and silent without song. But Pepicek,
the smallest child in the village, gathered the
children together and marched singing into the
woods, freeing the birds and routing the wicked
Ludvik. (In the pantomime a group of children
chase HONZA about the stage.) The lesson?
Alone, we are helpless. Together we are not
afraid of Ludvik--or of anyone. (The children
sing. The following words can be put to almost
any folk song.)

CHILDREN.

>   Ludvik, the Carpenter, warning we bring
>   you.
>   Children of Cheb come to claim stolen
>   song.
>   Close both your ears while our merry
>   songs sing you:

> Marching together we'll drive you along.
> Out of our village we'll run you and rout
>   you,
> Freeing our birds from your cages and
>   bars.
> Children together we don't fear to flout
>   you,
> Standing together the victory is ours.

(They sing. Bells ring. Ludvik comes into the
scene and the children sing loudly. They begin
to chase him and he runs off. The refrain of the
song keeps returning and dies away as Ludvik
disappears. The final notes wind down to
silence.)

RAJA (as she turns, smiling in remembrance,
    from the scene). Ludvik--with the rehearsals,
    the performances--was our hope. We could not
    let it die. The transports carried away children
    to die--new children took the empty places but
    Ludvik stayed and the children found strength
    and courage in playing their parts in it. (She
    listens to the last strains of music in the dis-
    tance. She looks out over the audience quickly
    as if she recognizes someone in the group.) I
    know a game. I'll bet that lady with the little
    girl over there will turn around. Or maybe that
    gentleman. . . . I hum a motif from Ludvik,
    and no matter where they are, they hear it.
    That would not work with anyone else. . . . (She
    hums a motif, and waits. Then as from a great
    distance, she hears the melody repeated.) You
    can try it anywhere in the world. Just hum a
    motif from our opera, and you will find them.
    They are sure to come--the few who remember
    Terezin. (Train sounds come up. Over the
    loudspeaker, RAJA hears the names of the
    children.)

LOUDSPEAKER. Eva Heska, 14 years old, perished at Auschwitz. Ela Hellerova, 13 years old,
perished at Auschwitz. Hanus Hachenburg, 14
years old; Petr Fischl, 15 years old; Marika
Friedmanova, 12 years old; Frantisek Bass, 14
years old; perished at Auschwitz. Bedrich
Hoffman, 12 years old; Josef Pollak, 14 years
old; Dita Valentikova, 13 years old; Nina
Ledererova, 14 years old; perished at Auschwitz. Eva Steinova, 13 years old; Hana Lissauova,
15 years old; perished at Auschwitz. Honza Kosec
. . . (Train sounds up.)

(Lights come up on RAJA, seated. She seems
wounded and stunned by the names she hears.
When she hears HONZA'S name, she runs to
the edge of the lighted area, searching the
darkness. HONZA can be heard, but not seen.)

RAJA. Honza?
HONZA. Raja . . . don't--don't turn or move.
RAJA (trying to locate the voice). Honza, where
are you?
HONZA. Don't move. Here, on the other side of
the wall--don't move, don't--just listen. I have
a number in this transport.
RAJA. No! (She searches the darkness for him,
moving on hands and knees.)
HONZA. Please--don't turn, don't move. . . . I
have a number and . . . I must report . . .
RAJA. No!
HONZA. But the news is good. . . .
RAJA. What do you mean?
HONZA. The war is coming to an end. . . .
RAJA. Honza . . . no!
HONZA. Things are going bad for the Nazis--

something will happen before long. . . . Raja,
please, listen. . . .

RAJA. Honza . . . where are you . . . I'm coming with you.

HONZA. You can't . . . it's too late. You must
wait here.

RAJA (quieter, but intensely). I cannot. . . .
Where are you?

HONZA. No . . . you must wait . . . for me.

RAJA (angrily). Honza, I cannot live waiting. . . .
Please, please, where are you, where are
you . . . (Pleading with him.)

HONZA (tenderly). I am with you--wherever you
are. . . . Listen, Raja. . . .

RAJA (vanquished). I'm listening. (She stares
unseeing into the darkness.)

HONZA. I have something. I never told you--
about the poem. I wrote one too, for the con-
test, remember?

RAJA (dazedly). You never handed it in . . .

HONZA. It was supposed to be about a memory,
only it's about you . . .

RAJA. You never told me . . .

HONZA. I'll leave it here, under the post near the
corner. Read it some time . . . but . . . don't
laugh . . . you laughed once at the other poem,
remember?

RAJA. I remember.

HONZA. When you read this . . .

RAJA. I won't laugh . . . I won't. I promise. . . .
Honza. . . . (She starts to move toward the
darkness.)

HONZA. Don't, don't, don't come out here. The
guards . . . Just stay there, stay there, and
wait. Good-bye. . . . (He leaves.)

RAJA. Honza . . . Honza? . . . Good-bye. . . .
(She walks to the edge of the area and finds the

sheet of paper. She reads, and HONZA'S voice
is heard reading with her.)
> Memory, come tell a fairy tale
> About my girl who's lost and gone,
> Tell, tell about the golden grail
> And bid the swallow, bring her back to me.
>
> Fly close to her and ask her soft and low
> If she thinks of me sometimes with love,
> If she is well? Ask too before you go
> If I am still her dearest, precious dove.
> And hurry back, don't lose your way.
> So I can think of other things.

(RAJA stops reading and HONZA'S voice continues.)

HONZA.
> But you were too lovely, perhaps, to stay.
> I loved you once. Good-bye, my love.

RAJA (folding the paper very slowly, carefully).
Good-bye. It was the motto of Terezin. It
should have been written over the entrance instead of the lie that greeted newcomers: "Work
makes us free." It was good-bye, not work,
that made us free. It was the only thing we
knew would never change. Good-bye . . . good-
bye . . . good-bye. It freed us all. What was
there to fear when you had said good-bye to
everyone you ever loved?

(Lights come up on IRENA, ready for transport.
She puts a shabby jacket over her shoulders and
sits down with a stub of a pencil to write a note.
Her voice is heard as she writes.)

IRENA. Raja, Raja Englanderova, you know by now
that my number--102866--was called; when you
come to school today you will see that I have

gone. You will have questions, and I will answer them before you ask. Once I saw an old
Bible picture. Satan was about to pierce a saint
through with his lance. The saint was sitting
comfortably there, as if it had nothing to do
with him. I used to think that the medieval
painters were incapable of presenting feelings
like fear, astonishment, or pain--so it looked
as if the saints had shown no interest in their
own martyrdom. Now I understand the saints
better: what could they do? (She rises and goes
to the side where she enacts the following.) I
have wrapped up the last of the pictures and
poems in my shawl. See that these are buried
with the rest--somewhere. And remember what
they mean to all of us. I have nothing else to
give you but this--what you and all the children
have made of Terezin--the fields, the flowers--
and all the butterflies. . . . Good-bye. . . .
(She, IRENA SYNKOVA, places the rolled package tenderly near the letter. She leaves with a
last look. The light stays up on this last remembrance of Terezin, then slowly dims to
black.)

(RAJA steps out of the darkness into the light. The
sack she left at the beginning is there.)

RAJA. Irena Synkova, perished at Auschwitz,
January 28, 1945. . . . And I have survived.
Mother, Father, Pavel, Irca, Zdenka--Honza.
Irena, too, in the end, perished at Auschwitz
and I, Raja Englanderova, after the liberation
returned to Prague--alone, alone.

(A dim light comes up on a GROUP standing upstage
huddled in the background. As the lights grow

brighter, they turn, each addressing RAJA in a
quiet voice as if from a great distance. Music
under the montage of voices. On the projection
screen, paintings, pictures . . .)

CHILD II.
> For seven weeks I've lived in here,
> Penned up inside this ghetto,
> But I have found my people here. . . .

IRENA. Now you are not alone. And you must not
be afraid.
FATHER. We will return. You will see, somehow,
we will return. . . .
CHILD I. I missed Daddy, yesterday, but I didn't
give in to my sadness. . . .
CHILD II. Some Polish children are coming. We
are making toys and little bags and nets for
them. . . .
CHILD III. I went to look for Zdenka. She cried
and laughed at the same time, she was so happy
to see someone before she left. . . .
IRCA. I believe in life--I and Pavel . . .
IRENA. Now you are not alone. You must not be
afraid. . . .
RABBI. Yes, yes, I will marry you, if you wish
to go together. . . .
HONZA. I never understood, until my father, dying, told me: "You are a good boy, Honza. You
are afraid, but you are not a coward. . . . "
IRENA. Somehow one of us is sure to survive.
One of us will teach the children how to sing
again, to write on paper with a pencil, to do
sums and to draw----
CHILD I.
> He doesn't know the world at all
> Who stays in his nest and doesn't go out.

He doesn't know what birds know best,
Nor what I want to sing about,
That the world is full of loveliness.

(Music: Snatches of chorus from Ludvik.)

HONZA. Raja . . . I am with you--wherever you
     are . . .
RABBI. As they walk through the Valley of Sorrow,
     they make it a place of springs.
IRENA. I have nothing else to give you but this . . .
     the fields, the flowers, and all the butterflies.
     . . . (As the voices grow in intensity, RAJA
     turns to view the people who have called to her
     from the past. She speaks to each.)
RAJA. Mother, Father, Pavel, Irca, I hear you.
     Honza, I hear and I remember. . . . Irena
     Synkova, I taught the children. (She picks up
     the sack and adjusts her coat. She pushes up
     the sleeve of the coat and looks at a number on
     her arm, then determinedly, pulls down her
     sleeve. She faces the audience again.) My name
     is Raja--I am a Jew; I survived Terezin--not
     alone, and not afraid. (She walks slowly across
     the stage. Music, creating the determined,
     strengthened mood of her liberation. Suddenly,
     butterflies are projected on the screen in the
     back, on the floor of the stage, everywhere.
     The whole stage is bright with color, moving
     with butterflies, as RAJA walks off, leaving
     the butterflies alive before the audience. Lights
     dim to black as music rises.)

THE END

PRODUCTION NOTES

1. The play was written to be performed without intermission.

2. Although the first production of this play utilized various theatrical media to reproduce Raja's past, the play can be done quite simply without such technical devices. Perhaps the only essential sound effect is the train, since it sets the mood and establishes the tense and expectant atmosphere of life in a concentration camp.

3. This is basically a memory-play, narrated by Raja. The actions she remembers, the sounds she hears, take on reality for her--and for the audience.

4. There are three acting areas on the stage, each area defined only when the lights come up on it. The first area represents the present, in which Raja stands, and from which she moves freely in and out of her past, as represented by the other two areas.

5. Although the Cast calls for only four children, there can be as many children and young people as desired. The young people who play Honza, Erika and Renka, Pavel and Irca might also double in some of the classroom scenes, since some of the poems and drawings were the work of adolescents.

6. There is an abundance of music in public domain available as background music. The well-known motif from Smetana's Moldau is the basis of the Czech national anthem. A variation of the theme is also used in the national anthem of the State of

Israel. As such, it makes a good evocation of both the Czech and Jewish elements in the play. Almost any collection of Czech or Hebrew folk songs will contain enough varied simple songs from which to draw music for the many moods of the play.

PROPERTIES

GENERAL: Various steps and platforms, stools.

RAJA: School bag; bundle containing tattered clothing, a book, a small box, and an identification tag, all wrapped in a black shawl; small package containing a sausage.

IRENA: Sheaf of odd-sized papers; shabby jacket, paper, stub of pencil, rolled package of papers.

MOTHER: Sabbath candles, matches, wedding ring on finger.

AUNT VERA: Glass, kerchief.

CHILDREN: Drawing and writing materials.

WEDDING GROUP: Ritual canopy, cup of wine.

HONZA: Sheet of paper (camp newspaper), poem written on sheet of paper.

DIRECTOR'S NOTES

DIRECTOR'S NOTES

DIRECTOR'S NOTES

DIRECTOR'S NOTES

DIRECTOR'S NOTES